HEINEMANN
Profiles

Steven Spielberg

An Unauthorized Biography

Sean Connolly

Heinemann Library
Chicago, Illinois

© 1999 Reed Educational & Professional PublishingPublished by Heinemann
Published by Heinemann Library,
an imprint of Reed Educational & Professional Publishing,
Chicago, Illinois

Customer Service 888-454-2279

Visit our website at www.heinemannlibrary.com

Designed by Visual Image

Printed in Hong Kong / China

03 02 01

10 9 8 7 6 5 4 3

Library of Congress Cataloging-in-Publication Data

Connolly, Sean, 1956-
  Steven Spielberg / Sean Connolly.
    p.   cm. — (Heinemann profiles)
  Filmography: p.
  Includes bibliographical references and index.
  Summary: Presents the childhood, career, and family life of the
motion picture producer and director Steven Spielberg.
  ISBN 1-57572-694-7 (lib. bdg.)
    1. Spielberg, Steven, 1947- —Juvenile literature. 2. Motion
picture producers and directors—United States—Biography—Juvenile
literature. [1. Speilberg, Steven, 1947- . 2. Motion picture
producers and directors.] I. Title. II. Series.
PN1998.3.S65C68 1998
791.43'0233'092—dc21
  [b]   98-7466
                                                                CIP
                                                                 AC

Acknowledgments

The Publisher would like to thank the following for permission to reproduce photographs: All Action
Pictures, p. 49; Aquarius Library, pp. 18, 26, 28 (bottom), 30; Susan Roper Arndt, p. 16; BFI Stills,
Posters and Designs, pp. 20, 23, 34, 38, 44; Corbis-Bettman, pp. 10, 40, 47, 48, 51; Pacha, p. 4, Reuters,
p. 45; UPI, p. 36; Ronald Grant Archive, pp. 25, 28 (top), 31, 39, 43; HHPFT/Science and Society
Picture Library, p. 12; Richard Y. Hoffman, Jr., pp. 7, 9; Loretta Knoblach, p. 8; Kobal Collection, pp. 14,
32, 33, 37, 41; Moviestore Collection, pp. 22, 46; Robert Opie, p. 35.

Cover photograph reproduced with permission of Rex Features.

Every effort has been made to contact copyright holders of any material reproduced in this book.
Any omissions will be rectified in subsequent printings if notice is given to the Publisher.

Any words appearing in the text in bold, **like this,** are explained in the Glossary.

This is an unauthorized biography. The subject has not sponsored or endorsed this book.

CONTENTS

WHO IS STEVEN SPIELBERG? 4

CHILD OF THE SUBURBS 6

HOME MOVIES 10

A TASTE OF SUCCESS 14

A HELPING HAND 18

IN AT THE DEEP END 20

BREAKING FREE 22

NOW FOR THE BIG SCREEN 24

SHARK ATTACK! 26

LOOK TO THE SKIES 30

FAILURE AND SUCCESS 32

TRIUMPH AND TRAGEDY 34

WEARING TWO HATS AGAIN 38

NEW HORIZONS 40

TOWERING ACHIEVEMENTS 42

COUNTING HIS BLESSINGS 46

STILL DREAMING OF SUCCESS 48

THE CHANGING VIEW OF
   STEVEN SPIELBERG 50

THE MOVIES OF STEVEN SPIELBERG 52

GLOSSARY *54*

MORE BOOKS TO READ *55*

INDEX *56*

Who Is Steven Spielberg?

Steven Spielberg is the world's most successful
moviemaker. Hundreds of millions of people
around the world have seen his movies, which include
two of the most popular movies of all time: *Jurassic
Park* and *E.T. :The **Extraterrestrial***. It sometimes seems
that everything he touches turns to gold, but Spielberg
has had his share of mistakes and failures as well.

Master of technique

Spielberg is known mainly as a **director** of movies.
He is able to guess how audiences will react to a
scene in a movie. He is skilled in making a movie
excite, sadden, or amuse people as they watch it.

**Steven Spielberg
plans a shot on
the set of Lost
World: Jurassic
Park, 1996**

This skill, particularly when it is repeated in the making of movie after movie, is rare, and Spielberg is greatly admired for this ability to touch the audience. Spielberg's movies communicate a childlike wonder about the world around him.

PERSONAL REFLECTIONS

Spielberg understands **suburban life,** television, and fast car technology, all of which became more common in his childhood in the 1950s. Movies such as *Jaws* and *Close Encounters of the Third Kind* succeed because they are about ordinary people, even though they are involved in extraordinary events.

As his career has developed, however, Spielberg has been able to touch on even deeper aspects of his past. As a child, Spielberg's Jewish background exposed him to the darker side of human nature. Other children often treated him as an outsider, and he was the only Jewish child at his school. Touching on this experience, he went on to direct *Schindler's List*, his impressive account of the **persecution** of the Jews during the Second World War.

Directing is 80 percent communicating and 20 percent know-how.

Steven Spielberg, 1987

Just how did this young American director from the suburbs become such a success?

CHILD OF THE SUBURBS

Steven Allan Spielberg, the oldest child of Arnold and Leah Spielberg, was born in Cincinnati, Ohio, on December 18, 1946. The Spielbergs were Jewish, and Steven's first memories—when he was only six months old—were of being wheeled in a baby carriage down the aisles of the local **synagogue**, with bearded men appearing as shadows against a bright light. Steven's awareness of his Jewish heritage would play an important part in his life.

In different ways, each of Steven's parents would also have a deep influence on the young boy's upbringing and character. Arnold was an electrical engineer and was interested in computers, which had just been developed at the time of Steven's birth. Leah, on the other hand, was the artistic parent. She had given up a promising career as a concert pianist when she married and settled down.

The Spielbergs' other children were all girls: Anne, Sue, and Nancy. As the four children grew older, they would become playmates, finding fun in each other's company each time the family settled in a new neighborhood. Arnold's job meant that they often had to move to different parts of the country. The first move in 1949 was to Haddonfield, New Jersey. The journey took them from the Middle West to the bustling East Coast of the United States.

In his early teens, Steven became a Boy Scout, enjoying the companionship and teamwork that came from scouting activities.

When Steven was six, his father took him to Philadelphia to see his first movie, *The Greatest Show on Earth*. Steven enjoyed this exciting circus story, but a few things puzzled him about this new experience. At first he could not understand how a circus could perform on a flat screen, and part of him felt disappointed that he couldn't smell the sawdust and gunpowder.

The Spielbergs' house in New Jersey, like millions of suburban homes across the United States, was built in the years immediately following World War II.

In 1954 the family moved again, this time to Scottsdale, Arizona, a **suburb** of Phoenix in the desert country of the Southwest. Steven, who was already showing signs of being a sensitive child, was upset by the move, although his mother painted a picture of the exciting times that lay ahead.

Being a stranger in a new school was also difficult. Steven was a slow reader and not very good at the games the other children played. Once he and 50 of his classmates went on a mile run. After a while, all the runners had completed the course, except for Steven and John, a mentally handicapped boy. The other children cheered John on, and Steven deliberately slowed his own pace so that the other boy would cross the finish line first. The crowd carried John away on their shoulders while Steven remained on the track crying.

Steven was not good at games, but this was not the only reason for his feelings of isolation. He was the only Jewish child at school, and some of the other children made spiteful remarks about this. The worst came when a group of schoolchildren gathered in front of the house and shouted, "The Spielbergs are dirty Jews! The Spielbergs are dirty Jews!"

Arnold Spielberg accompanied Steven (center) and other Boy Scouts on trips into the Arizona mountains.

HOME MOVIES

Scottsdale was in many ways a typical American **suburb** in the 1950s. People lived in single-family houses, tended small gardens, played ball, and had barbecues. Children would go to each other's houses to play or ride their bikes around the neighborhood.

Steven's own sensitive character, combined with the teasing that he often received at school, meant that for him none of these normal activities was very exciting.

Television was still a novelty in the 1950s, and the whole family would sit and watch.

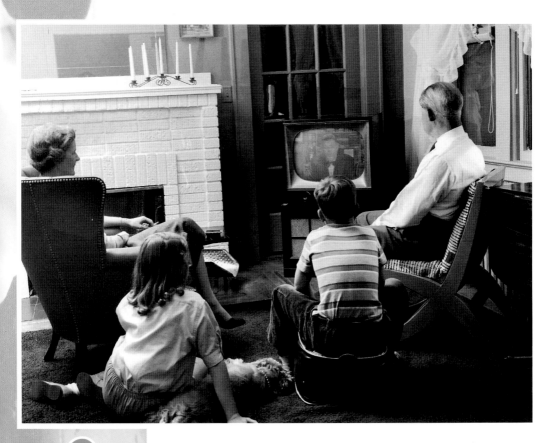

AN EARLY PRODUCTION

Instead, he made his own entertainment, often at the expense of his younger sisters. He convinced them that he had a dead World War II pilot rotting away in his bedroom, and he dared them to go and take a look. When it was dark, he took them into his room quietly, opened his closet door, and shone his flashlight on a plastic skull wearing a helmet. Steven, a skillful showman, loved his success as his sisters ran away screaming.

Some early influences

As a child in the 1950s, Steven Spielberg was influenced by watching movies and television. His parents took him to the theater to see action movies such as *Davy Crockett* and the Walt Disney classics *Bambi*, *Fantasia,* and *Snow White*. Just as important, though, were the many hours he spent watching television. Steven's parents insisted that he watch only children's programs such as *The Mickey Mouse Club* and *The Atomic Club*. When they went out Steven would sneak down to watch some of the forbidden grown-up programs. These included exciting police shows (*Dragnet* and *Highway Patrol*), comedies (*The Honeymooners* and *Soupy Sales*), and eerie fantasy programs (*Science Fiction Theater*).

When Steven was about seven years old, he developed a taste for television, despite the attempts his parents made to control the children's viewing. When his parents were out, Steven would wait until the baby sitter had fallen asleep and then creep downstairs to watch television. But first, he had to deal with the booby trap that his father had laid, a secretly-placed hair on the television "On" switch. Steven would memorize the position of the hair and always replace it exactly where he had found it after watching hours of police dramas, comedies, and old movies.

The Kodak 8 mm movie camera was portable enough to take anywhere.

Eventually a chance came for Steven to combine his mischievous ability to entertain with his love of television. When Steven was twelve, Leah Spielberg gave her husband an 8 mm Kodak movie camera for Father's Day. Arnold's first efforts were terrible—he images wobbled and were usually out of **focus**. Irritated by his son's constant teasing and criticism, Arnold handed Steven the camera and said "why don't you try?"

Steven proved to be a natural with the camera. He used his toys as characters and began making small adventure movies. By his teens, Steven had made his first short movie, called *The Great Train Crash*, in which he had used his own model railway. Steven's parents were amazed at how lifelike this "disaster" appeared. They might not have realized it, but Steven was also perfecting important film techniques such as **continuity** and **composition**.

DEVELOPING A GIFT

Before long the Spielberg house began to look like a movie set, with furniture and lights constantly being moved around to prepare for a new movie. Steven was not shy about using his sisters' toys in some of his productions; even today they must have mixed feelings about *The Terror of the Burning Doll's House*.

The movie camera was Steven's constant companion. He filmed the family at home and on vacation, particularly during their hiking trips in Arizona. Steven constantly worked on his self-taught technique, but his early efforts show how much he was helped by his parents' influence. His vivid imagination and choice of subject matter reflected his mother's artistic nature, but Steven's emphasis on accuracy and precision came from his father.

A Taste of Success

The famous director John Ford poses on the set of *The Man Who Shot Liberty Valance* with his stars, Hollywood legends James Stewart *(left)* and John Wayne, (1962)

"Mom, we're shooting tomorrow," Steven would say, and that would be enough for his mother to abandon plans to have friends over for coffee or to practice her own music. By the time Steven had reached his early teens, the Spielberg house looked more and more like a miniature film **studio**. Floodlights strung together with thick electric cables shone down on the family rooms. Mountains made of papier-mâché acted as backdrops for the scenes being played. And overseeing it all was Steven, camera held to his eye, always on the lookout for the best shot.

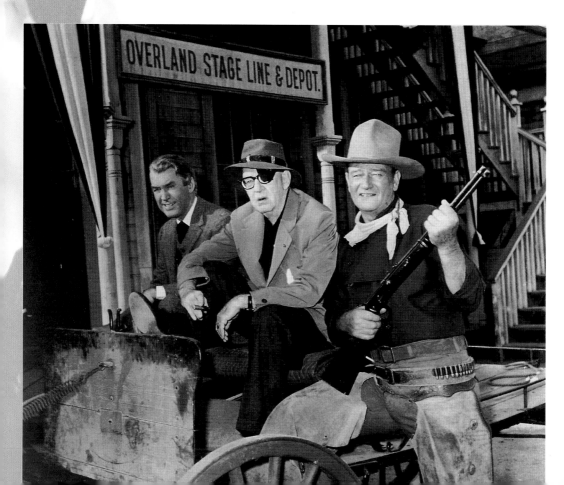

Moviemaking had become Steven's life, and he spent the summer vacations doing odd jobs for neighbors in order to earn money for new equipment. He even rented movies and showed them at home, with his mother and sisters selling popcorn and soft drinks to his classmate customers.

School became better for Steven now that he had such fun at home. He began shooting movies with actors and even used his filmmaking skills to stop some of the bullying that he got at school. One boy, who had previously made life difficult for Steven, became the star of a forty-minute war movie, *Battle Squad*. The boy enjoyed it and became a good friend.

A PERSONAL TOUR

Hollywood, with its busy movie studios, remained Steven's dream. He was able to follow that dream in 1963 during a summer vacation in California with his cousins. Like thousands of other tourists, Steven bought a ticket for the guided tour at Universal Studios. But as everyone else boarded the tour bus, he hid, and then began exploring on his own. He wandered onto sets and even met the famous **director** John Ford. One film editor was so impressed with the young visitor that he handed him a one-day pass. Steven waved the pass at guards and decided to do the same thing every day for the rest of the summer.

American Artist Productions

PRESENTS

World Première
OF THE MOTION PICTURE

FIRELIGHT

Phoenix Little Theatre

MARCH 24, 1964
8:00 P.M.

Special programs were printed for *Firelight*, Steven Spielberg's first real movie, which showed a confidence and skill far beyond his years.

Steven hoped that the film world would be impressed with the short movies that he packed in his briefcase, but the reaction at Universal was only lukewarm. Still, the film bug had definitely bitten, and when Steven returned to Arizona, he borrowed $400 from his father and began making a **feature-length** movie.

A REAL MOVIE

The new project was a science fiction movie called *Firelight*, a tale about UFOs that attack Earth. Although Steven was only 16 years old, he persuaded student actors from Arizona State University to act in it. He even convinced the local airport to close down a runway for one scene. The length was as ambitious as the plot; the finished movie ran 140 minutes.

Arnold Spielberg hired the local Scottsdale movie theater for one night, and *Firelight* had its world premiere on March 24, 1964. When Steven examined the **box-office** take, it showed that the public had spent $500 on tickets. The movie had made a $100 profit.

Steven was lucky to have met the sometimes cranky John Ford when the **director** was in a sunny mood. Ford even gave Steven some practical tips about film-making, which ended with the most important advice, "Never use your own money to make a movie."

A Helping Hand

Steven did not have much time to savor the one-night success of *Firelight*. The next day, the family moved to Saratoga, a suburb of San Jose in northern California. Steven had to settle into a new school again. At Los Gatos High School, he had to put up with vicious **anti-Semitic** comments in the halls. There were constant threats of violence, so for the last six months of high school, Steven was picked up by his parents at the end of each day.

A convenient college

Because Steven's grades at school had been only average, he could not attend the university of his choice. He wanted to enroll at the prestigious film school of the University of California at Los Angeles.

Spielberg enrolled at California State University in 1965, but his studies were cut short by his film ambitions.

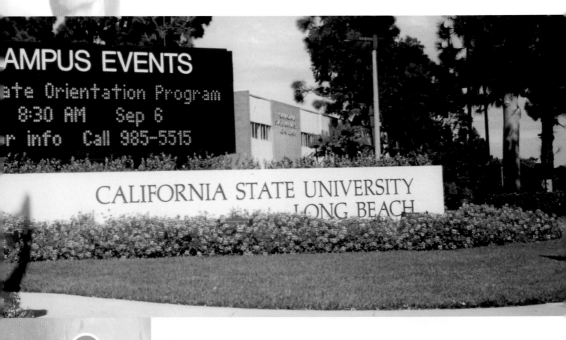

Instead, he chose to study English at California State University at Long Beach. At least this choice of university would bring him physically closer to **Hollywood.**

BACK TO THE STUDIO

While Steven was a student he began spending three days a week back at Universal Studios. Again he watched experts at work, and once more he tried to impress the film people. His determined attitude and enthusiasm finally paid off when he met a young man named Denis Hoffman, who ran a company that produced **special effects** for movies. Hoffman offered Spielberg the chance to direct a short movie, called *Amblin'*, about a boy and girl who meet in the California desert and hitchhike to the Pacific Ocean.

The movie had no words but used a **soundtrack** performed by musicians who had business links with Hoffman. *Amblin'* was completed in the late summer of 1968 when Steven was just 21 years old. The **negative** of the 24-minute film was stored in a laboratory at Universal Studios. It would prove to be a lucky omen for Steven, because *Amblin'* was going to be a lucky charm in his dealings with the great **studio**.

IN AT THE DEEP END

After all the years Steven Spielberg had spent dreaming about getting into **Hollywood**, his breakthrough came almost in an instant. Chuck Silvers, a Universal Studios editor who had met Spielberg, persuaded Sidney J. Sheinberg, president of Universal's television department, to watch *Amblin'*. Sheinberg was impressed and arranged a meeting with Spielberg. He was convinced that Spielberg had the talent to become an accomplished **director,** and he offered him a seven-year contract. Spielberg decided to give up college and take the deal, which was signed within a week.

Still in his early 20s, Spielberg (left) had to direct Hollywood stars such as Joan Crawford.

THE YOUNG PROFESSIONAL

At just 22 years old, Steven Spielberg was given his first professional assignment: to direct an episode from the television series *Night Gallery.* In keeping with the spooky nature of the series, the plot was about a wealthy, but blind, woman who pays a fortune to be able to see for a short time. The sting in the tale comes when there is an electrical blackout just as she regains her sight.

Spielberg relished the challenge and used many of the directing techniques that he had learned or developed over the years. But this was the first time that he had to direct professional actors, and one of the stars was Joan Crawford, once one of the leading lights in Hollywood. There were delays in shooting, and afterward Spielberg was disappointed to learn that much of the episode had been reworked to get rid of his "fancy" techniques.

More television experience

Despite the bumpy start, Spielberg soon learned to provide what the television executives wanted. He did more work on *Night Gallery* as well as on other series. One of his favorites was "LA–2017," an episode of the series *Name of the Game.* The episode, in which the star is hit on the head and wakes up in the twenty-first century, gave Spielberg the chance to indulge his love of science fiction.

Amblin' to success

Just as Spielberg's television career was beginning to take off, he got another boost. *Amblin'* was entered in various film festivals and won the Silver Phoenix Award at the 1969 Atlanta Film Festival. Years later Spielberg recognized the importance of this short movie when he set up his own production company, naming it Amblin Entertainment.

BREAKING FREE

While working for Universal, Spielberg found that television put many limits on the type of ideas he wanted to explore, both in subject and technique. He began to worry about losing the enthusiasm that had taken him so far. Could he find a way around this problem?

The answer came with the TV movie *Duel*. Spielberg read the **screenplay** and convinced Universal executives that he could tell the story of a man terrorized on the open road by a huge truck. The man and the audience never see the driver of the truck, which adds to the suspense. Spielberg used some of the techniques that were discouraged in the other television programs. He also used tricks from the famous "Road Runner" cartoons. Just as the driver thinks he has outrun the truck, it appears once more, ready to attack. The suspense builds throughout the film until the truck finally plunges over a cliff and bursts into flames.

Dennis Weaver, the star of *Duel*, portrayed an ordinary guy, a type of hero that would appear in later Spielberg films.

The sprawling expanse of Universal Studios is as large as a small town. *Duel*, broadcast on ABC Television in the United States in 1971, proved to be one of the most popular TV movies ever shown. Universal bought the film back from ABC, got Spielberg to film new sequences, and then distributed it outside the United States. Spielberg traveled to Europe to help **promote** *Duel* and to accept an award from a film festival in Sicily. He made a special trip to Rome to meet Federico Fellini, the great Italian film **director** whose name alone was enough to sell his films.

American TV

Steven Spielberg was fortunate to perfect his filmmaking skills at a time when each episode of some popular American television programs told its own story, much like a movie itself. These were good experience for the young director. As well as *Night Gallery* and *Name of the Game*, Spielberg directed episodes of *Marcus Welby, M.D., Owen Marshall, Counselor at Law,* and he even directed the first episode of the extremely popular detective series *Columbo*, starring Peter Falk.

Now for the Big Screen

With the success of *Duel*, both on television and in international theaters, Spielberg had shown that he could carry a full-length movie from the planning stage to the finished product. And for the big **Hollywood studios**, the most important thing was that the finished product made a good profit. Now Spielberg wanted to make movies that were planned for theater release in the first place.

A FALSE START

Spielberg approached the task with patience and determination. He was offered the chance to direct *White Lightning*, a thriller starring one of Hollywood's most popular actors, Burt Reynolds. Spielberg spent three months preparing for this job, looking at **locations** and agreeing on a **cast**. Later, he decided that the movie was never going to be anything special, and it might stop his career just as it was starting, so he chose to drop the project.

EXCITEMENT ON WHEELS

Finally, Spielberg convinced Universal to let him film *The Sugarland Express*, which was based on the true story of a Texan woman and her escaped convict husband who try to regain **custody** of their baby. The movie was extremely difficult to make, largely because most of the plot centered on a thrilling car chase across Texas.

William Atherton (left) and Goldie Hawn play the runaway couple who kidnap a policeman in The Sugarland Express, 1974.

The "express" of the title is the ever-growing line of cars following the fugitives, including police cars, news reporters, and excitement-seeking onlookers.

The Sugarland Express turned out to be an exciting movie, with twists in the plot mirroring the twists, turns, and flips of the speeding cars. Unfortunately, two similar films had recently appeared on American movie screens, so its success was limited. Spielberg had another reason for the movie's relatively poor performance: he tried to tell too many stories at once and the plot got confused. In his next movie he would tell one big story without being sidetracked.

And what a story it turned out to be.

Although *The Sugarland Express* was not a full commercial success, it caught the eye of many film critics. One of these critics, Pauline Kael of the influential *New Yorker* magazine, even said: "In terms of the pleasure that technical assurance gives an audience, *Sugarland* is one of the most phenomenal debuts in the history of movies."

Shark Attack!

Even before *The Sugarland Express* had been released, Steven Spielberg had lined up his next project. In the summer of 1973 he read the **galley proofs** of *Jaws*, a novel that was about to be published. Spielberg was fascinated by this tale of a coastal town being terrorized by a great white shark, and he decided that he would like to direct it. "I wanted to do *Jaws* for hostile reasons," he said later. "I read it and felt that I had been attacked."

The successful **Hollywood producers** Richard D. Zanuck and David Brown owned the **film rights** to the novel *Jaws,* and Spielberg used all his powers of persuasion to convince them to let him direct the movie version. They finally agreed, and the movie went into the planning stage with Spielberg at the helm.

The beach scenes in Jaws (1975) captured the sense of the swimmers' panic when they learn that a killer shark is just offshore.

Spielberg had clear ideas about how the novel should be made into a movie. He wanted to concentrate on the basic conflict between the ordinary people and the brute force of nature, so he cut some of the less exciting dry land parts out of the screen version. Then, after spending many hours watching *20,000 Leagues Under the Sea, Moby Dick,* and other sea movies, Spielberg decided that *Jaws* must be filmed on **location**, without using **studio** water tanks to mimic the look of the sea.

The technical crew chose Martha's Vineyard, an island off the coast of Massachusetts, as the ideal location. The island was big enough to accommodate a large film crew, and it had water at least 35 feet (10.5 meters) deep, with a flat sandy bottom.

Filming began in the summer of 1974. What neither Spielberg nor his crew had anticipated were the crowds of vacationers and the hundreds of small boats that seemed to be drifting into every scene. Also, the weather was changeable—a constant problem for **continuity**—and treacherous currents could sweep away expensive equipment or even one of the stars. In fact, they lost two cameras, and Spielberg himself was once swept overboard.

The young **director** had to keep a firm grip on every aspect of the filming schedule. He kept a close eye on the **cast**, making sure they were comfortable and happy, and tried to limit the number of sightseers who showed up each day on the set. Most importantly, Spielberg became an expert at handling the difficult controls of "Bruce," the 23 foot (7 meter) mechanical shark, saying it was "about as easy to operate as a 747.

Despite Spielberg's planning and skill, the movie began to fall behind schedule. Luckily for Spielberg, he was able to rely on storyboarding to help keep the last third of the filming schedule under control. He did not leave the island until the last scene was shot, 155 days after he had arrived.

An intricate system of levers and pulleys operated "Bruce," the mechanical *Jaws* (1975).

Storyboarding

Storyboarding, which Spielberg used to keep a grip on the production of *Jaws*, is a method of planning the way in which a movie is shot. The director breaks down the script into a number of detailed pictures, each of which represents the ideal frame of a particular scene. The director can indicate other things on the storyboard, such as where to point the cameras and how the actors should move within this frame. By solving many problems before shooting begins, storyboarding can save time and money later on in the schedule.

For years he just scared us. Now he gets to scare the masses.

Anne, Spielberg's sister, after seeing *Jaws*, 1975

My next picture will be on dry land. There won't even be a bathroom scene. Spielberg, 1975, acknowledging the difficulties of filming near the sea

The finished version of *Jaws* opened in movie theaters in the United States in spring 1975. The public loved it. The movie earned $7 million in its first three days of release and went on to earn over $260 million in the U.S. alone. This broke all existing records, and the 28-year-old director leapfrogged to the forefront of the film world.

What's the big idea?

Hollywood studios usually take great care before committing themselves to the expense of a new feature film. They usually look for movies with a "big idea," that is, an easily understood concept that drives the plot and holds the audience's attention from start to finish. *Jaws* passes the big idea test easily because its central theme of a killer shark terrorizing a vacation resort takes hold and never lets go—almost like a shark bite!

LOOK TO THE SKIES

Filming *Close Encounters* (1977) allowed Spielberg to work with one of his own heroes, the French film director Francois Truffaut *(center)*.

The record-breaking success of *Jaws* gave Steven Spielberg a great deal of power and influence within **Hollywood**. In particular, it meant that he could follow his own ideas for movies, knowing that he would almost certainly be able to direct the movie of his own choice. For his next movie, he looked upward as well as to his own past.

DEVELOPING THE IDEA

Spielberg's first long film, *Firelight*, made when he was only sixteen, developed one of his favorite themes, intelligent life in outer space. While he was making *Jaws*, he developed a story about Unidentified Flying Objects (UFOs). This first idea was titled "Watch the Skies" and concerned a U.S. Air Force officer who had to help the government pretend that there were no such things as UFOs. Columbia Pictures agreed to the idea, and Spielberg asked the screenwriters from *The Sugarland Express* to write the script, which became *Close Encounters of the Third Kind*.

The story revolves around a group of ordinary people who find themselves drawn to a mysterious mountain in the U.S. West. Once they reach it, they find a group of people waiting for a huge spaceship to land. The spaceship makes contact with them and—once it lands—aliens come out to welcome the humans on board, to go with them into space. The characters, like the audience, have no idea what to expect when they reach the spacecraft, but they are driven by unstoppable curiosity.

Publicity posters for Close Encounters captured the movie's sense of awe and mystery.

ANOTHER HIT

Close Encounters of the Third Kind was a gamble for Spielberg and Columbia, and its first reviews were negative. However, the movie-going public provided Spielberg with another **box-office** hit, increasing his power and influence within Hollywood. It seemed that Spielberg could not fail—or could he?

Spielberg and the Oscars

Steven Spielberg was nominated for the Best Director Academy Award for *Close Encounters.* These awards are the U.S. film industry's highest praise. Spielberg failed to win the **Oscar,** just as he had when *Jaws* had failed in its nomination for Best Picture. Many people wondered whether Hollywood was jealous of his success.

FAILURE AND SUCCESS

Spielberg, seen here with Robert Stack and Toshiro Mifune, tried hard to create a comic atmosphere in 1941.

Spielberg's films had always relied on the humor in everyday details, and so it was not surprising that he thought he could direct a comedy. In 1978 he set about making *1941*, a nonstop action comedy set in Los Angeles during World War II. This project, however, only showed Spielberg's limitations. He hired many of America's most popular comedians in the hope that their presence alone would make the movie funny.

BOMBS AWAY

The mix of constant explosions, plane crashes, and chaotic running around failed to find the audience's funny bone. Although *1941* made some money worldwide during its 1979 release, most people viewed it as a failure, although they might not have gone as far as the *Washington Post*, which described it as "an appalling waste of filmmaking."

BACK WITH A VENGEANCE

Upset and tired by the whole ordeal of *1941,* Spielberg gratefully accepted an offer of a vacation in Hawaii with his friend George Lucas, the **director** of *Star Wars*. There they came up with the story that would become *Raiders of the Lost Ark*.

Spielberg's good working relationship with Harrison Ford helped turn *Raiders of the Lost Ark* into box-office gold (1981).

Spielberg and Lucas were looking back to the same era as the events of *1941*, but they stayed within territory that they knew how to handle. They created the American hero Indiana Jones, who single-handedly takes on what seems to be half of Nazi Germany and outwits them. The movie and the hero are based on cinema **serials** of the 1930s and 1940s, with the plot building with a series of cliffhanging adventures. Spielberg directed the movie with just the right touch of humor and pace, and the finished product turned out to be the most successful American movie of 1981.

At 34, Spielberg was back where he felt happiest, able to work on his favorite projects.

Feelings of doubt

Spielberg had his doubts about whether *1941* would be a success, or even funny. Typically using a **Hollywood** comparison (from the film *The Wizard of Oz*), he admitted in 1978: "Yes. I'm scared. I'm like the Cowardly Lion, and two smashes back to back have not strengthened my belief in my ability to deliver."

TRIUMPH AND TRAGEDY

How much is the name Steven Spielberg worth when it appears above a movie's title? By the early 1980s the answer was millions, even hundreds of millions. Spielberg had wealth, power, and most important, creative freedom to choose or develop movie ideas. Sometimes he might be too busy to direct one of these movies, but his involvement, and more importantly, his credit as **executive producer**, would sell the movie.

E.T. was a complicated mixture of mechanics, electronics, and actors, including a mime artist and two dwarfs.

It was in these circumstances that Spielberg became involved with the movie *Poltergeist*. The idea for this story about poltergeists, playful ghosts, was Spielberg's, and he claimed to have written the **screenplay** in five days. The movie was directed by Tobe Hooper and showed all the signs of a Spielberg movie: it was about ordinary people coping with extraordinary events. The success of *Poltergeist*, however, was nothing like Spielberg's next project as **director**, which became the movie phenomenon of the 1980s.

A CLOSER ENCOUNTER

The heart-warming movie *E.T.: The* **Extraterrestrial** began as a possible **sequel** to *Close Encounters of the Third Kind.* Spielberg had asked screenwriter John Sayles to produce a screenplay that would recapture the sense of wonder of *Close Encounters of the Third Kind.*

The movie E.T. gave birth to products which earned $1 billion worldwide.

One of Sayles's main ideas was that an alien might be left behind by a departing spacecraft. The resulting story of how E.T. is befriended by Elliot, and later by his brother and sister, works like a fairy tale.

In directing this movie, Spielberg left behind his storyboarding technique. This gave him more scope to make changes to the filming plans on the spur of the moment. He put more of himself into the movie, remembering ideas that he had had since he was a child.

Audiences clearly shared these feelings of wonder, and the industry recognized Spielberg's ability to touch viewers as much as the greatest "family" directors before him. One critic summed this up by describing *E.T.* as "the best Disney movie that Walt Disney never made."

> I feel I'm still a kid. I'm 35 and I haven't really grown up yet.
> Steven Spielberg, 1982, the year of *E.T.*

A SUDDEN SHOCK

On July 23, 1982, just two weeks after the triumphant opening of *E. T.*, Steven Spielberg received some devastating news. Three actors, including two children, had been killed on the set of *Twilight Zone*, a movie that Spielberg was producing. A helicopter had gone out of control and crashed into the three actors. To make matters worse, the two children had been hired without permits. It was the law to have permits, which specify guidelines on working conditions for child movie actors.

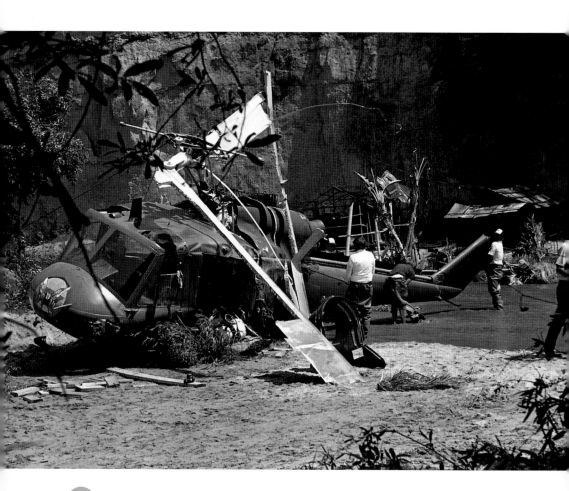

Twilight Zone was made up of four parts, each with a different director. Spielberg himself was directing one of the stories, but the accident happened in the part directed by John Landis. A series of investigations and a court trial followed. Landis and other crew members were eventually found not guilty of involuntary **manslaughter** in 1987.

Although neither Spielberg nor Warner Brothers faced any charges, the events of the tragedy continued to haunt Spielberg. Could he move forward if he dwelt endlessly on *Twilight Zone* and its effects?

Full circle

The *Twilight Zone* project meant more to Spielberg than some of the other movies he produced. It was a tribute to Rod Serling, a talented screenwriter of the 1950s and 1960s who presented a spooky television series of the same name. The Serling connection was a strong one for Spielberg. It was Serling who wrote *Night Gallery*, the first television job that Spielberg had completed back in 1969.

WEARING TWO HATS AGAIN

Director Joe Dante (*right*) welcomed Spielberg's comments and advice on the set of *Gremlins* in 1983.

fter the *Twilight Zone* tragedy, Spielberg went back to his known strengths: directing action blockbusters and making movies that reflected his own views of life. During 1983, he directed a second Indiana Jones movie, *Indiana Jones and the Temple of Doom*, and produced a movie called *Gremlins*.

TURNING THE TABLES

The Temple of Doom, described as a **prequel** to *Raiders of the Lost Ark*, received lots of publicity. But it was almost overshadowed by the second project. *Gremlins* concerned mischievous creatures that reminded audiences of *E. T.*, but the similarity soon ends. Cuddly and sweet at first, the gremlins change character when they are exposed to water.

The public loved watching a typical American small town descend into chaos as the creatures run riot. Eventually calm is restored, and the original gremlin is returned to the wise old Chinese storekeeper who first cared for it. The story ends with the old man explaining that "society without responsibility is society without hope."

One exciting
scene in *Indiana
Jones and the
Temple of Doom*
sent its stars
Harrison Ford
and Kate
Capshaw,
hurtling down a
mine shaft.

OVERDOING IT?

Indiana Jones and the Temple of Doom saw one of film's favorite heroes battling his way through adventures in China, Thailand, and India. Like *Raiders of the Lost Ark*, *The Temple of Doom* was an enormous commercial success.

The new movie, however, was criticized for the use of violence and for the way in which it seemed to show Asian people as shifty or evil. Spielberg was hurt by these criticisms. He tried to play down his involvement in the movie, describing himself as a "hired hand." He admitted that he would not allow a ten year old to see the movie: "The responsibility to the children of this country is worth any loss at the **box office**."

Perhaps the child in him was beginning to grow up. But would it show in any of his next movies?

NEW HORIZONS

S pielberg was at a crossroads by the mid-1980s. He wanted to be taken seriously by critics as someone who could deal with mature, adult issues. Perhaps success in that area would lead to an **Oscar**.

A NEW FAMILY

At this time, Spielberg's personal life changed. In the early stages of his career, he had thrown himself into his work, turning down invitations to parties and other social events, especially while making a movie. But in 1985, he married the actress Amy Irving. A son, Max Samuel, was born that same year. Spielberg's choice of movies also began to change. He directed *The Color Purple*, about a group of African-American women and the difficulties they face. The movie was quite successful, but the critics insisted that Spielberg had toned down the original novel in order to make a **mainstream** movie.

Spielberg and his wife, Amy Irving, attended many formal functions in Hollywood.

RISKS AND SECURITY

Because *The Color Purple* was successful, despite the critical reaction, it was felt that Spielberg could handle material that **Hollywood** considered risky. In 1986 Spielberg took on another risky project, a movie version of the novel *Empire of the Sun*.

Spielberg took great care to get just the right performances from Whoopi Goldberg and other cast members of *The Color Purple*, 1985.

The book, by British novelist J.G. Ballard, looks at the outbreak of World War II through the eyes of a young English boy who is living in China. Spielberg uses the study of human nature, rather than chases and explosions, to hold the audience's interest. The movie received mixed reviews, with Spielberg fans hating the movie and Spielberg critics praising it.

Spielberg returned to familiar ground for the third part of the Indiana Jones **trilogy**, *Indiana Jones and the Last Crusade*, made in 1989. Even the familiar "Indy antics" were given a new, more mature, slant and much of the movie's success came from the lively exchanges between Indy and his father, played by veteran star Sean Connery.

He gets physically ill when a project is over. The people involved become his family. He loves them and hates for it to be done and to leave everyone.

Anne Spielberg, sister

Towering Achievements

Spielberg's marriage to Amy Irving did not stand up to the strains of the couple's ambitious Hollywood lives. They divorced in April 1989. In October 1991, Spielberg married Kate Capshaw, who had starred in *Indiana Jones and the Temple of Doom*. Around the same time, Spielberg released *Hook*, a version of J.M. Barrie's much-loved book *Peter Pan*. The movie failed miserably, leaving Spielberg unable to make his mark on the new decade.

The roots of success

Few could have known that Spielberg would be able to do just that with his next two movies, which were hugely successful, and finally receive the highest critical praise.

In 1982 Spielberg had come across the novel *Schindler's Ark*. The novel tells the true story of Oskar Schindler, a German businessman who saved the lives of Jewish workers and rescued others from Nazi death camps during World War II. Remembering his own Jewish background, Spielberg became sure that the novel should be filmed. But who would direct such a powerful story?

Directing dinosaurs

That problem nagged Spielberg throughout the 1980s, but by the early 1990s he was certain that he

The animated dinosaurs of Jurassic Park (1993) were added after filming was completed.

could do the job, backed up by his production company, Amblin Entertainment. Spielberg showed the idea to Universal Studios. They agreed, as long as he would direct one of their projects first.

That project turned out to be *Jurassic Park*, the action-filled story of a dinosaur theme park where the animals break free. Spielberg and his crew did much of the shooting on the Hawaiian island of Kauai. Just as shooting was beginning, a fierce hurricane swept across the island, killing 3 people and leaving 8,000 homeless.

The filmmaking did go on when the rubble was cleared and finally the **location** shooting was completed. The only problem was that there were no dinosaurs at this stage—they were to be added later using high-tech **special effects**.

Exploring his soul

By now Spielberg had flown to Poland to work on *Schindler's List*. By day he shot scenes from the new movie, and in the evening he oversaw the **special effects** for *Jurassic Park*, which were sent by satellite from the United States. Spielberg's devotion to *Schindler's List* made it a classic full of excellent direction and fine performances from its **cast**.

He shot the movie in black and white, to add to the feeling that it was a documentary recording the events of the **Holocaust**. He remembered stories from his mother and grandfather as he filmed the tragic events of that brutal time. Slowly the movie began to reveal itself as a personal, deeply felt statement.

Spielberg personally chose actor Liam Neeson to play the lead role in *Schindler's List* (1993).

I mustn't use my Spielbergian bag of tricks here. I must simply eavesdrop with the camera, just tell the story, keep peeling that onion away, get very, very bare and stark.
Spielberg on his technique for *Schindler's List*

REAPING THE REWARDS

Both movies were released in 1993. *Jurassic Park* swept aside the previous record-breaking money earner, *E. T.*, and earned nearly $1 billion worldwide. Spielberg received about $40 million for his direction and earned even more from the many products that used the Jurassic Park name.

Spielberg earned less from *Schindler's List*, although that hardly mattered because the movie became an instant classic. There was almost universal praise for one of the best movies ever made. The icing on the cake came during the next Academy Awards ceremony, when *Schindler's List* won seven **Oscars**, including Best **Director** for Spielberg.

It should be noted … that Mr Spielberg has this year delivered the most astounding one-two punch in the history of American cinema.
New York Times film critic Janet Maslin, 1993

Counting his Blessings

For several years after *Schindler's List* and *Jurassic Park,* Spielberg took a break from directing. In many ways he had finally proved himself to audiences, critics, and most importantly, to himself. He still worked on other movies through his production company, Amblin Entertainment.

One good turn deserves another

Spielberg also had the chance to offer someone else some of the success and lucky breaks he felt he had received. As **producer** of the movie *Casper,* based on the cartoon series about a friendly ghost, Spielberg offered 30-year-old Brad Silberling a big break, just as Universal's Sid Sheinberg had done for him. Silberling had wanted to become a **director** after first seeing *Jaws.* Like Spielberg he had spent years with a home movie camera before getting a job in television. Spielberg liked what he saw.

Jeff Goldblum (left) was one of the Jurassic Park stars who returned in Lost World: Jurassic Park, (1997).

Spielberg has helped raise millions for the Survivors of the Shoah Visual History Foundation.

He offered him the director's job and provided moral support while the movie was being made. The movie went on to earn more than $100 million, leaving everyone happy with Spielberg's choice of director.

TWO VIEWS OF THE PAST

Spielberg found the ideal **"sequel"** to *Schindler's List*. He gave the millions of dollars he earned from the movie to the Survivors of the Shoah Visual History Foundation, a nonprofit organization devoted to recording the story of **Holocaust** victims and their families. Spielberg also helped to attract money from big business.

The sequel to *Jurassic Park* was more commercial. In 1997 Spielberg directed and released *The Lost World: Jurassic Park*. Although **box-office** sales did not reach the astronomical heights of the first movie, it swept the world on its release.

I cry every time I get involved in watching someone's story. But I don't turn away. If I do, what can I expect others to do?

Spielberg on his work with the Survivors of the Shoah Visual History Foundation, 1994.

STILL DREAMING OF SUCCESS

Steven Spielberg had long remembered the words of the veteran movie **director** John Ford: "Never use your own money to make a movie." That advice had seemed sound during the years when Spielberg was a relatively unknown director and no one was sure that his movies would make a profit. He earned a fee for each movie, which increased as a percentage of the movie's earnings as he became more successful. But the largest share of the profits went to the **studio**.

HOLLYWOOD'S NEWEST STUDIO

With this in mind, Spielberg and two business colleagues, Jeffrey Katzenberg and David Geffen, decided to set up their own studio. DreamWorks SKG was formed on October 11, 1994. Its aims are to make movies, television programs and records.

Spielberg relaxes with DreamWorks SKG partners Jeffrey Katzenberg and David Geffen.

The team of founders knows that Spielberg's name sells movies, but they also know that big gambles can lead to equally big losses. No one knows this risk more than Spielberg himself. Another such risk is his 1998 movie *Amistad*, which is about a slave **revolt** in the 1800s.

Spielberg the family man enjoys time at home as much as making movies.

A GROWING FAMILY

As well as having a new team at work, Spielberg has a growing team at home, his wife and children. His family now includes seven children: two from his marriage to Kate Capshaw, one from Capshaw's previous marriage, one from Spielberg's marriage to Amy Irving, and three adopted children. The family grew particularly during the three-year break Spielberg took from directing after *Jurassic Park* and *Schindler's List*. With such company and support at home, it seems likely that Spielberg will be able to explore his theme of childlike wonder for many years to come.

I'd like to be able to tell my child that it's all like it is in the movies. That we always slay our dragons, wake up from our nightmares, and that it's easy to tell the good guys from the bad guys. Steven Spielberg, 1997

The Changing View of Steven Spielberg

From the start of Steven Spielberg's career, he was praised as a skillful technical **director**. This meant that he knew how to shoot or edit a scene in order to get the audience to shriek, gasp, or sigh in relief. *Jaws* made people scream, *E.T.* brought tears to the eyes, and *Jurassic Park* made audiences gasp in amazement. But did this increasingly successful filmmaker have anything more to offer?

Victim of his own success

Even some of Spielberg's closest colleagues felt that he was more of a commercial director than one with any particular artistic skill or depth. Sid Sheinberg, who had discovered the young Spielberg and who bought the **film rights** to *Schindler's List*, considered Spielberg a popcorn director without the necessary intelligence to direct that terrible tale of Nazi horror.

Such a view was common, and for many years Spielberg seemed to be like a bright child who needs the approval of the grown-ups around him. For Spielberg, the grown-ups are the movie critics, who in many ways are the judges of a director's reputation.

Growing up in public

Since the 1980s, Spielberg has tried to explore new themes and sometimes failed in his attempts.

Steven Spielberg cut the ribbon at the grand opening of the Universal Studios Florida theme park in June 1990. Some critics praised Spielberg, listing *The Color Purple, Empire of the Sun,* and even *Always,* a romantic comedy, for their growing understanding of human nature.

With *Schindler's List,* this process was completed. Having set off on his film journey by showing the ordinary person in difficult circumstances, Spielberg showed that he could explore the very nature of humanity itself.

Stanley Kauffman, of the influential *New Republic magazine,* summed up Spielberg's remarkable career in 1993: "Spielberg has done the best directing of his career. Much of his previous work has been clever, but *Schindler's List* is masterly…a welcome astonishment from a director who has given us much boyish **esprit**, much **ingenuity**, but little seriousness. His stark, intelligent style here perfectly controlled, suggests that this may be the start of a new period in Spielberg's **prodigious** career—Part Two: the Man."

The Movies of Steven Spielberg

Feature-length movies directed by Steven Spielberg

Duel (Universal, 1972)

The Sugarland Express (Universal, 1974)

Jaws (Universal, 1975)

Close Encounters of the Third Kind (Columbia, 1977)

1941 (Columbia/Universal/A-Team, 1979)

Raiders of the Lost Ark (Paramount/Lucasfilm, 1981)

E.T.: The Extraterrestrial (Universal, 1982)

Twilight Zone—The Movie (Warner Brothers, 1983)

Indiana Jones and the Temple of Doom (Paramount/Lucasfilm, 1984)

The Color Purple (Warner Brothers/Amblin/Guber-Peters, 1985)

Empire of the Sun (Warner Brothers/Amblin, 1987)

Indiana Jones and the Last Crusade (Paramount/Lucasfilm, 1989)

Always (Universal/United Artists/Amblin, 1989)

Hook (Tristar/Amblin, 1991)

Jurassic Park (Universal/Amblin, 1993)

Schindler's List (Universal/Amblin, 1993)

Lost World: Jurassic Park (Universal/Amblin, 1997)

Amistad (DreamWorks SKG, 1998)

Feature-length movies with Spielberg as executive producer

I Wanna Hold Your Hand (Universal, 1978)

Used Cars (Columbia, 1980)

Continental Divide (Universal, 1981)

Poltergeist (MGM, 1982)

Twilight Zone—the Movie (Warner Brothers, 1983)

Gremlins (Warner Brothers/Amblin, 1984)

Fandango (Warner Brothers/Amblin, 1985)

The Goonies (Warner Brothers/Amblin, 1985)

Back to the Future (Universal/Amblin, 1985)

Young Sherlock Holmes (Paramount/Amblin, 1985)

The Money Pit (Universal/Amblin, 1986)

An American Tail (Universal/Amblin, 1986)

Innerspace (Warner Brothers/Amblin/Guber-Peters, 1987)

Batteries not included (Universal/Amblin, 1987)

Harry and the Hendersons (Universal/Amblin, 1987)

Who Framed Roger Rabbit? (Touchstone/Amblin, 1988)

The Land Before Time (Universal/Amblin, 1988)

Back to the Future II (Universal/Amblin, 1989)

Dad (Universal/Amblin, 1989)

Back to the Future III (Universal/Amblin, 1990)

Gremlins II — The New Batch (Warner Brothers/Amblin, 1990)

Joe Versus the Volcano (Warner Brothers/Amblin, 1990)

Arachnophobia (Hollywood Pictures/Amblin, 1990)

An American Tail II —Fievel Goes West (Universal/Amblin, 1991)

Cape Fear (Universal/Amblin, 1991)

Noises Off (Touchstone/Amblin, 1992)

A Far-off Place (Touchstone/Amblin, 1993)

We're Back! A Dinosaur's Story (Universal/Amblin, 1993)

The Flintstones (Universal/Amblin, 1994)

Casper (Universal/Amblin, 1995)

The Little Rascals (Universal/King Features/Amblin, 1995)

How to Make an American Quilt (Universal/Amblin, 1995)

To Wong Foo, Thanks for Everything, Julie Newmar (Universal/Amblin, 1995)

The Bridges of Madison County (Warner Brothers/Amblin, 1995)

Balto (Universal/Amblin, 1996)

Twister (Universal/Warner Brothers/Amblin, 1996)

GLOSSARY

anti-Semitic targeting Jewish people as the object of insults or violence

box office front of the theater where tickets are sold. It also describes the total amount of money earned through the sale of tickets for a movie.

cast actors who play the roles in a movie

composition way in which the director arranges the images that appear on the screen

continuity how scenes in a movie follow naturally from one to another

custody the legal right to care for a child

director person who supervises all aspects of how a movie is made (acting, scenery, lighting and music) to make sure the movie works as it is intended

esprit a lively intelligence

executive producer person who is finally responsible for the business matters and production of several movies, while each movie also has its own **producer**

extraterrestrial coming from outside Earth, usually a creature who comes from outer space

feature-length long enough to be the main feature at a theater

film rights legal rights to adapt a play, novel, or short story into a movie

focus adjustment of a camera lens so that the objects being filmed appear clearly and are not blurred

footage particular length of motion picture movie, which is wound around reels and can be measured by the foot; usually describes a sequence of a film

galley proof one of the pages supplied to an author or publisher in order to check for mistakes before a book is printed

Hollywood area in Los Angeles, California, which is the center of the American movie business. Hollywood can also be used as a general term to describe commercial American movies.

Holocaust systematic slaughter of millions of Jews in Nazi camps during World War II (1939–1945)

ingenuity intelligence with inventiveness

location place where a movie is being shot outside rather than inside a **studio**

mainstream appealing to a wide range of audiences by being easy to understand and by avoiding any offense

manslaughter unintentional killing of another human being

negative original film obtained from the camera when filming was done

Oscar (also known as an Academy Award) one of a group of statuettes awarded annually by the American Academy of Motion Picture Arts and Sciences for professional achievement in motion pictures

persecution causing harm to a group because of its beliefs, race, or religion

prequel an invented word (using "**sequel**" as its root) to describe a story that concerns events that occurred before the action that takes place in another story

prodigious large size or amount

producer person who is responsible for raising money for a movie as well as hiring the crew that will work on it. It is up to the producer to ensure that the film does not fall behind schedule and that it is delivered on time.

promote advertise and generally make sure that a movie receives a great deal of publicity in order to attract large audiences to it

revolt rise up against a power or government

screenplay movie or television script that describes the plot of a story and includes instructions for the filmmaking team

sequel follow-up to a successful story or movie, retaining many of the characters from the first story

serial movie, radio, or television program that appears regularly, usually each week

soundtrack the sound and music that is recorded to accompany the visual images of a film

special effect unusual visual or sound effects that cannot be produced through normal filming. Special effect artists use computers, enlarged photographic images, models, and other devices to simulate natural disasters and science fiction sequences

studio room that is specially equipped for making a movie or other recording, or the buildings and land that a company needs to make movies

suburban concerning a small residential community outside a city or town

synagogue Jewish place of worship

trilogy series of three related books, plays, or movies

MORE BOOKS TO READ

Knight, Bertram. *Steven Spielberg: Master of Movie Magic.* Morristown, NJ: Silver Burdett Press. 1998.

Meachum, Virginia. *Steven Spielberg: Holywood Filmmaker.* Springfield, NJ: Enslow Publishers. 1996.

Powers, Tom. S*teven Spielberg: Master Storyteller.* Minneapolis, MN: The Lerner Publishing Group. 1996.

INDEX

California State University 18–19

Capshaw, Kate 39, 42, 45, 49

Crawford, Joan 20, 21

Disney, Walt 11, 35

DreamWorks SKG 48

Fellini, Federico 23

Ford, Harrison 33, 39

Ford, John 14, 15, 17, 48

Geffen, David 48

Holocaust 44, 47

Hollywood 15, 20, 24, 26, 29, 30, 33, 40

Irving, Amy 40, 42, 49

Katzenberg, Jeffrey 48

Lucas, George 32–3

Martha's Vineyard 27

Night Gallery 20, 21

Oscars 31, 45

Scottsdale, Arizona 8, 10, 12

Serling, Rod 37

Sheinberg, Sidney J. 20, 50

Silberling, Brad 46

Spielberg, Arnold and Leah 6, 9, 12, 45

Spielberg, Steven
  and television 11, 12, 20–1, 22–23
  childhood 6–13
  on being Jewish 5, 6, 9, 18, 42, 44
  films as director
    Always 51
    Amblin' 19, 21
    Amistad 48
    Close Encounters of the Third Kind 5, 30–1, 35
    Color Purple, The 40–1
    Duel 22–3

Empire of the Sun 40–41

E.T.: The Extraterrestrial 4, 34–5

Firelight 16–17

Hook 42

Indiana Jones and the Last Crusade 41

Indiana Jones and the Temple of Doom 38–9

Jaws 5, 26–9

Jurassic Park 4, 43–4

Lost World: Jurassic Park 47

1941 32

Raiders of the Lost Ark 32–33

Schindler's List 5, 42, 44–5, 47, 50

Sugarland Express, The 24–5, 30

Twilight Zone—The Movie 36–37

  films as producer
    Casper 46
    Gremlins 38
    Twilight Zone—The Movie 36–37
    Poltergeist 34
  home-movie making 12–13
  marriage and family 40, 42, 49

storyboarding 29, 35

Survivors of the Shoal Visual History Foundation 47

Universal Studios 15, 17, 19, 20–22, 23, 43, 51